The Wonder of
CHEETAHS

To my grandchildren, Marlon and Melodie
—Winnie MacPherson

Please visit our web site at: www.garethstevens.com
For a free color catalog describing Gareth Stevens Publishing's list of high-quality books
and multimedia programs, call 1-800-542-2595 (USA) or 1-800-461-9120 (Canada).
Gareth Stevens Publishing's Fax: (414) 332-3567.

Library of Congress Cataloging-in-Publication Data

Lantier, Patricia.
    The wonder of cheetahs / by Patricia Lantier and Winnie MacPherson; illustrated
by John F. McGee.
        p. cm. — (Animal wonders)
    Includes index.
    "Based on . . . Cheetah magic for kids . . . by Winnie MacPherson"—T.p. verso.
    ISBN 0-8368-2763-5 (lib. bdg.)
    1. Cheetah—Juvenile literature. [1. Cheetah.] I. MacPherson, Winnie, 1930-
II. McGee, John F., ill. III. Title. IV. Series.
QL737.C23L363   2001
599.75'9—dc21
                                                    00-053818

First published in North America in 2001 by
Gareth Stevens Publishing
A World Almanac Education Group Company
330 West Olive Street, Suite 100
Milwaukee, WI 53212 USA

This edition is based on the book *Cheetahs for Kids,* text © 1998 by Winnie MacPherson, with
illustrations by John F. McGee, first published in the United States in 1998 by NorthWord Press,
(Creative Publishing international, Inc.), Minnetonka, MN, and published in a library edition as
Cheetah Magic for Kids by Gareth Stevens, Inc., in 2000. Additional end matter © 2001 by
Gareth Stevens, Inc.

Photographs © 1998: Stephen J. Krasemann: Cover; Erwin and Peggy Bauer: 26, 38-39; Craig
Brandt: 7; Dembinsky Photo Associates: Fritz Polking: 8, 13, 22, 24-25, 30, 34, 40; Adam Jones:
14; Mike Barlow: 42; Mark J. Thomas: 47; Len Rue, Jr.: 10-11, 28-29; Art Wolfe: 16, 18-19, 21.

Printed in the United States of America

1 2 3 4 5 6 7 8 9 05 04 03 02 01

The Wonder of
CHEETAHS

by Patricia Lantier and Winnie MacPherson
Illustrations by John F. McGee

Gareth Stevens Publishing
A WORLD ALMANAC EDUCATION GROUP COMPANY

AFRICA

Serengeti

The fastest land animal in the world lives on the continent of Africa. It hunts in open grasslands such as the Serengeti wildlife refuge.

The fastest land animal is also very beautiful. Do you know what it is?

The cheetah! Cheetahs are beautiful mammals with short, golden fur and black spots. They have a small head, a large chest, a slender body, and powerful legs.

Cheetahs are members of the cat family. They are carnivores, which means they eat only meat.

Cats such as lions and tigers hide and pounce to catch prey. Cheetahs use their lightning speed.

They can run
at speeds up
to 70 miles
(115 km)
per hour.
Cheetahs
are the
champion
sprinters
of the cat
family.

Cheetahs are cautious animals. They like to keep a close watch over what is going on around them. They sit in high places, such as in trees, on large rocks, or even on termite mounds. Cheetahs are especially cautious when their babies are close by.

Cheetah means "spotted one." The animal's black spots and golden fur blend into the long grasses of the Serengeti. The two black stripes on their faces also help them hide in the grass.

Cheetahs have excellent eyesight. They can see their prey or enemies, even when they are far away.

Cheetahs also hear very
well. By moving their
ears around, they hear
prey before they see it.

Baby cheetahs are called cubs. Like adults, cubs have spots and stripes. Their fur, however, is long and gray until they are about three months old.

Cubs stay in a lair until they are about six weeks old. The lair is usually under a bush. Even when cubs are very young, a mother cheetah will leave them alone while she goes hunting. Her cubs' long, fluffy fur helps hide them from predators when she is away.

When the cubs are about six months old, mother cheetahs teach them to hunt — but they are still too young to hunt large prey.

When cubs get too close to strangers, they spit at them and try to look ferocious.

Cheetah cubs
are always
hungry. Their
mothers must
hunt every
day to feed
the family.

When a mother cheetah takes her cubs on a hunt, she guides them through the tall grasses with the tip of her long tail.

Cheetahs hunt during the day, and they often need to get out of the hot sun. They usually look for shade under trees or under the bushes of their lairs.

When young
cheetah
brothers leave
their mothers,
they often
stay together.
As a group,
they can catch
more prey
than if they
hunt alone.

Cubs must learn how to stalk and hunt prey as well as protect themselves from predators. They know how to hide from enemies in the tall grasses. They also know that they must stay alert and quiet when predators are close by.

Unlike other big cats, cheetahs do not roar. Cheetahs chirp, squeal, yelp, bark, growl, and purr. Some of these sounds are used to warn other cheetahs of danger. Female cheetahs often purr loudly while washing or feeding their cubs.

Cheetah cubs have lots of energy. Fighting playfully helps them develop the skills they will need to hunt prey. They also learn how to defend themselves. Cubs roll around in the grass and take turns hiding and jumping on each other.

Cheetah cubs roll around, nip each other on the back or neck, and chase each other in a circle. Sometimes mother cheetahs join in the fun. A mother cheetah is very patient with her cubs, even when they tug on her tail or jump at her face.

When prey is near, a mother cheetah gives her cubs a signal to hide. Then she uses her lightning speed to catch their dinner.

Prey watch cheetahs carefully and rush away if a cheetah runs toward them.

Cheetahs are fast because they are light. Five cheetahs weigh as much as one lion.

Cheetahs have sleek bodies. Adults weigh only 100 to 130 pounds (45 to 60 kg). They have small heads and

narrow teeth. Their mouths have no space for big front teeth like other cats have.

Small, tough pads on the bottoms of their feet grip the ground like sneakers when cheetahs run.

A cheetah's backbone is like
a spring. It gives the cheetah
a powerful push when it
runs or jumps.

Long, thick tails help cheetahs
keep their balance when they
are chasing prey.

Cheetahs can run at full
speed for only a minute or
two. They must catch prey
quickly, before they get tired.

After they capture prey, cheetahs must hide it so other predators will not steal their food. Hyenas, jackals, and lions all steal food from cheetahs.

Then cheetahs rest. After they have rested, cheetahs can finally eat.

Not many animals are as beautiful as the cheetah. If you see one, look quickly — they are *fast!*

Glossary

carnivorous — meat-eating

lair — the home or shelter of a wild animal

mammals — warm-blooded animals that feed their young with mother's milk

pounce — to jump or swoop down suddenly

predators — animals that hunt other animals for food

prey (n) — animals that are hunted by other animals for food

refuge — a place of safety; a protected area

species — a group of animals or plants with similar characteristics

sprint — to run at top speed for a short distance

stalk — to track or follow in a quiet, secretive manner

Index